TAKING CARE OF BUSINESS

101 WAYS TO KEEP YOUR CUSTOMERS COMING BACK (WITHOUT WHINING, GROVELING OR GIVING AWAY THE STORE)

■

DICK SCHAAF RON ZEMKE

QUANTITY SALES

Most Lakewood books are available at special quantity discounts when purchased in bulk by companies, organizations, and special-interest groups. Custom imprinting or excerpting can also be done to fit special needs. For details write: Lakewood Books, 50 South Ninth Street, Minneapolis, MN 55402 or call (612) 333-0471.

■

LAKEWOOD BOOKS
50 South Ninth Street
Minneapolis, MN 55402
(612) 333-0471

Publisher: Philip Jones
Production Manager: Brenda Owens
Designer/Production Editor: Helen Gillespie
Cover Design: Kathleen Timmerman

10 9 8 7 6 5

Lakewood Publications, Inc. publishes *TRAINING Magazine, The Training Directors' Forum Newsletter, Creative Training Techniques Newsletter, Positive Employee Practices Newsletter, Potentials In Marketing* and *Presentations Magazine.*

Dick Schaaf, Vernacular Engineering,
P.O. Box 19316, Minneapolis, MN 55419; (612) 895-5330.

Ron Zemke, Performance Research Associates,
Suite 1820, Foshay Tower, 821 Marquette Avenue South,
Minneapolis, MN 55402; (612) 338-8523.

ISBN 0-943210-07-0

TABLE OF
CONTENTS

Customer Retention
in the 1990s

We know getting close to the customer is the key to building a successful business in today's service-centered, service-driven economy. We're learning (often the hard way) that it costs five times as much money to attract a new customer as it does to retain a customer we already have. We've heard how service has to be part of selling and how the need to build long-term, mutually satisfying customer relationships is the new Holy Grail of American business.

Yet, for all the brave talk about customer service, the real reason for the concern — customer retention — is often addressed only in passing, if at all.

Make no mistake: The idea of customer retention gets to the heart of building a successful business in the '90s. The key to success is not having customers. It's having customers *again*. To succeed, you have to bring them back. Loyal customers are an asset no competitor can steal so long as you protect them — and the future of your own business — by meeting, managing and sometimes exceeding their needs and expectations.

That's where quality service comes in. In an era where everything from automobiles and credit cards to retail stores and business-to-business services have become commodity offerings, quality really is the key. Quality products backed by quality services, or the lack thereof, are what distinguish you from your competitors. It's what causes customers to come back again — or decide to try to find someone who does pretty much what you do, but maybe just a little better.

Just as manufacturing businesses have discovered the profound impact of a commitment to quality in every aspect of their operations, today a service business must manage *service* quality for its long-term impact on the customer. You have to see your customers as a resource who must be carefully developed and smartly managed, never squandered or wasted. And you have to see your business as a constantly evolving system for satisfying customers again and again

In the pages that follow, we identify 10 broad areas that can be productively combined for customer retention. Within each, we provide capsule summaries of 10 effective tactics. Whether you adopt just one of them, or all 101, you'll find you needn't bust the budget or burn the midnight oil. Taking care of customers literally means taking care of business. You work to get a little bit better at all the various things you do.

Wondering how 10 strategies multiplied by 10 tactics can equal *101* ways to retain customers? Good. You're ready for ... Tactic #101: Pay Attention. To keep bringing your customers back, you need to learn from everything you see, hear, read or experience. Good ideas come from a wide variety of sources. But if you're not looking for them, if you're not keeping track of each and every little detail, you won't recognize them.

Good service is the end product of all the big and little things your business does for its customers. From their standpoint, everything counts. Keep them satisfied and they will come back. What's more, they'll not only keep you in business, but put you way ahead of your competition. And without making you whine, grovel or give away the store.

It all depends on the way you take care of business.

Dick Schaaf & Ron Zemke
Minneapolis
June 2, 1991

STRATEGY 1:
KNOW YOUR CUSTOMER

You must constantly be on top of changing customer needs and expectations. If your information is older than 90 days, chances are it is already becoming out of date.

1. Determine Customer Needs *And* Expectations

2. Master Customer Needs

3. Track Customers As They Change

4. Visit Customers On *Their* Turf

5. Prospect For Information Of Value

6. Solicit Information From Your People

7. Subscribe To Trade Publications

8. Keep Information Fresh

9. Keep In Touch

10. Build A Real Relationship

1

Determine Customer Needs *And* Expectations

Customers have both needs and expectations: The *substance* of what they want and need done and a *style* in which they expect it to be done. A physical performed by a rude, clumsy, smelly doctor will not be satisfying, no matter how competent the medicine being practiced, any more than an inept physical administered by a courtly, courteous clone of Marcus Welby, M.D.

According to author and service expert Leonard Berry of Texas A&M University, customers determine their satisfaction by weighing three factors — what they *expect* to happen, what actually happens, and what they observe of the process in between. All three play important roles in their determination of whether they received what they wanted ... and want to come back again.

Suppose you need to go to Cincinnati. The plane takes off on time. The inflight service is wonderful, the seat comfortable, the food the best you've ever had at 30,000 feet. But the plane lands in St. Louis. If you don't get where you're going, it won't matter how pleasant you find the ride. You won't be happy. No amount of "value added" service will make up for the wrong outcome.

It's easy to pay so much attention to how you're doing things that you lose sight of what it is you absolutely have to do to satisfy the customer. But if you're not able to consistently meet your customers' basic needs, you won't satisfy their basic expectation that you can indeed do what they need done. That's why companies from giants like 3M to small local firms increasingly define service quality as *"conformance to customer requirements."*

2

**Master
Customer
Needs**

3

Track Customers As They Change

To serve your customer well, it's not enough to just meet immediate needs. You have to know where you fit into the picture long-term, *anticipating* changes so when customers realize they need something new or different, you're ready to accommodate them. To do that, you need to understand what your customers do, how they are changing, and sometimes even who *their* customers are.

Trend researchers look for indications of incremental change as well as radical departures from known conditions. That's how Procter & Gamble spotted the need for All-Temperature Cheer and why restaurants now routinely offer non-smoking sections and decaffeinated coffee. The McDonald's axiom is, "We lead the industry by following our customers."

When customers do business with you, they often must do it on your premises or through your systems. You get, at best, an incomplete view of who they are and how they operate. Taking time occasionally to go out and visit them can give you important insights into their personal needs, their corporate character and how they use your goods and services.

Federal Express drivers are encouraged to look for materials from other delivery businesses to identify new services for their customers. Jim Miller, chairman of Texas-based Miller Business Systems, and his son Mike, the company's president, visit more than 200 of their office supply customers in the Dallas-Fort Worth area each year to find out more about the companies with which their company does business. Could it be only coincidence that they're number one in their markets?

4

Visit Customers On *Their* Turf

5

Prospect For Information Of Value

Supplement the time you spend seeking information by enlisting other sources to look for information of special value to you. Using key customers as search words, subscribe to a clipping service and explore online databases. Encourage your people to copy and route information that covers changing market conditions and customer needs. Circulate clippings that mention your customers and their competitors, or that provide useful information. To build the noncommercial side of your customer relationship, pass the information along to them, too.

In the process, learn to be selective. Access to information is not the problem today. Management is. Most businesses are drowning in information, and no one has the time to keep up on every subject that might be germane to current and future operations. A customer focus helps you prioritize.

Frontline people are a major untapped resource for market research in many organizations. Make them your eyes and ears. Nordstrom salespeople keep detailed files on their regular customers so they can recall in an instant what different people like or want. Barbers and beauticians use similar systems to "remember" the individual preferences of hundreds of customers. Tapping into that kind of information will give you insight no generalized study can hope to mimic.

Sharing frontline information at the frontline can have powerful results. At Walt Disney World and American Express, frontline workers meet every week or two to compare notes on experiences, problems, tough questions and customer perceptions. Combining individual impressions into insightful pictures of changing needs and expectations keeps your people focused on customers.

6

Solicit Information From Your People

7

Subscribe To Trade Publications

To keep yourself — and your people — informed about your industry, make sure trade publications, periodicals and newspapers are available to your staff. Encourage them to use these resources to stay current about their customers' businesses as well as their own. Make a point of reading them yourself so you can discuss "current events" (and reinforce the point that you believe in staying on top of changing conditions).

Once current issues have been circulated, collect them in a small, readily accessible corporate resource room (a *library*) where sales, service and management people can brush up on major stories and catch up on market trends. If space is at a premium, there's no need to be a packrat: Most of the information you need will be in the issues from the last 12 to 24 months.

The task of knowing your customer is one that is never over. Yet it's amazing (maybe appalling is a better word) how many businesses make crucial strategic decisions on the basis of market research and customer account data that's a year or two old. Technology changes constantly. So do financial and market conditions. So do customers. Key people come and go, or stay but in a different job. Competition, economic conditions and even world events can have ripple effects in unexpected places.

That doesn't mean you have to confront customers and frazzle your staff with eight-page forms as a condition of doing business. Instead, combine continuous frontline impressions and after-sale and after-service follow-μps with more formal research to keep a continuing reading on customer experiences and attitudes.

8

Keep Information Fresh

9

**Keep
In Touch**

"Out of sight, out of mind" is a five-alarm warning when it comes to developing lasting customer relationships. If the only memorable contact your customers have with you is the arrival of a periodic bill, or obvious and impersonal form letters, they'll soon begin to see you only as a line-item on the expense ledger.

Relationships have milestones and significant events that grow even more meaningful when they are remembered and acknowledged. Send greetings and congratulation cards to customers for new product launches, company anniversaries, promotions and the like. If you know your customer well enough, remember personal occasions, such as birthdays and anniversaries, too. Business relationships, like personal ones, thrive on constant communications.

10

Build A Real Relationship

Once, the sales process was akin to the proverbial one-night stand: You wooed. You won. You moved on in search of the next conquest. No more. Today, smart businesses build long-term relationships with their customers — and train and reward their people for making those relationships work day after day, week after week, year after year.

Beyer Volvo of Falls Church, VA, holds "mixers" so customers can meet the mechanic assigned to their car's needs. The airlines pioneered frequent flyer programs as a way to build and reward brand loyalty and repeat traffic, and the tactic is now used by hotels, restaurants, clothing stores, dry cleaners, bookstores, video rental shops and a host of others. Find ways to make your own business' customer relationships visible. And valuable.

STRATEGY 2:
MAKE YOURSELF
'EASY TO DO BUSINESS WITH'

Your business should be designed to make it easier to do things for the customer, not harder. If you hear your people telling customers things like, "You have to understand the way we do business around here," you are not being easy to do business with — and you may never see that customer again.

11. Be *Open* For Business

12. Be Open Even When You're Not Open

13. Advertise Your Hours

14. Handle The Call Volume

15. Install An 800-Number

16. Simplify Physical Layouts

17. Simplify Bills And Invoices

18. Let Customers Customize Your Support Systems

19. Listen To Yourself Saying "No"

20. Don't Leave Customers Hanging

11

Be *Open* For Business

Your business hours should reflect the times people want to do business with you. If you're locking the doors in the face of arriving customers, you're locking out their money — this time and maybe forever — and giving them visible evidence of just how much their business means to you.

A growing number of businesses, from grocery stores and automobile repair shops to doctors and dentists, conduct operations 12, 16, even 24 hours a day to be available to customers around town as well as around the globe. Flextime schedules and staggered shifts allow you to staff beyond the basic nine-to-five day. Remote terminal systems — such as ATMs and computerized diagnostic centers — make it possible to serve customers at all hours and no matter where they happen to be.

In today's economy, the hours most businesses are open are also the hours most potential customers are at work. But needs don't restrict themselves to the hours between nine and five. When your customer needs you after hours (or before), on a weekend or a holiday, do you have a system in place to respond? Don't let the clock limit your business by driving customers away.

A phone recording announcing your hours and instructing the caller to try again when it's convenient for *you* is not a customer-friendly system. Instead, use special night numbers or recorders that can take a message and be triggered from a remote location. Doctors have answering services to track them down for true emergencies. Savvy service providers make a point of writing their home phone number on business cards — or have them printed that way. You can, too.

12

Be Open Even When You're Not Open

13

Advertise Your Hours

Don't assume that your customers have memorized your hours of business, especially if you've extended them to nonstandard times. If they just assume you close shop when everyone else does, they've rendered a potentially strong competitive advantage useless. If you're open at special times, or at different times in certain seasons or on specific days of the week, make sure your customers know it.

And don't just post hours on the front door — get them into your customer's hands, too. Customer-focused businesses make a point of printing their hours (plus their name and phone number) on *anything* that a customer might refer to at a later date: bills, envelopes, packaging, advertising flyers, phonebook listings, refrigerator magnets ... and the product itself.

Customers hate busy signals and spending long minutes in phone queues. They resent being forced to listen to prerecorded sales pitches — or music (and especially commercials) from systems relaying radio station broadcasts they wouldn't choose to listen to at home or in their car. They may also chafe at long, involved prerecorded messages that run them through an electronic Skinner box of button-pushing before they make contact with a live human being.

Invest in telephone equipment that makes your business sound and act responsive and friendly. Make sure you have adequate phone lines and enough well-trained people to answer them. If you can't answer a call by the third or fourth ring, use an electronic back-up system to tell callers you'll be right with them. And if you're using direct numbers, publish your own phone book for customers.

14

Handle The Call Volume

15

Install An 800-Number

If you're drawing customers from outside the local telephone dialing area, give them a toll-free number to call for product and service information, to place orders, to complain, or to praise. If volume is heavy enough, have several and segment them to reflect customer types or needs. The expense is a modest investment vs. the sales you lose because a competitor is more reachable than you are. Don't overlook the value of a toll-free fax line as well — customers today communicate in a multitude of ways.

Be wary of 900-number service, which charges the customer for calling you. Abuses, ranging from monstrous (and unexpected) bills to disreputable soft porn and "gab lines," have given 900-number prefixes a bad name. And customers may quickly become sensitive to this additional cost of doing business with you.

Department stores are notorious for putting the "Customer Service" desk in the most remote, far-from-the-door location possible. Businesses do the same thing internally by putting valuable support services several floors away from the people who need them. Is your business designed with the customer's convenience in mind, or from an outside architect's artificial concept of order?

Design your physical layout for efficiency and effectiveness, not pointless aesthetics. Use signage, lighting, directories and other cues to help customers figure out where they're supposed to go. Make your services physically accessible, not only to wheelchairs, but to older customers (America's population is aging steadily). Pay attention to lost or bewildered customers: Their confusion will help you find and fix chronic trouble spots.

16

Simplify Physical Layouts

17

Simplify Bills And Invoices

A constant pet peeve of customers of virtually all businesses, but especially service businesses, is that they're not sure exactly what they're paying for. People who feel mystified by your cost formulas or powerless without someone to decipher a bill or warranty for them will wonder whether they're really getting their money's worth.

When in doubt, ask your customers what they like and what they would change. Ther design your financial statements and other documentation around that information. Use plain English, not jargon and legalese. And don't miss the chance to inform and educate them, or solicit feedback. Emerald People's Utility District in Eugene, OR, offers a space for comments on the remittance copy of each monthly bill so customers can voice a concern, ask a question or offer a compliment.

As long as you're going to define service quality as conformance to customer needs and expectations, why not assure literal conformance? If a few customers would rather have you bill on the 20th of the month instead of the 15th, or want electronic records dumped to their database, customize your own systems to accommodate them.

Dataserv, a computer systems maintenance service, sets up each customer's account individually, from billing dates and formats down to allowing customers to help select members of the account team. GTE North, a GTE subsidiary providing residential telephone service in the Midwest, asks customers when they would like the repair tech to come out to install or fix the phone. With predictable regularity, most say, "I don't know. When can you be here?" (But research shows they appreciate being asked.)

18

Let Customers Customize Your Support Systems

19

Listen To Yourself Saying 'No'

Policy, more than one pundit has pointed out, is the first response of the vested bureaucrat. Sometimes there are valid reasons for denying a request — McDonald's would be as ill-advised to serve McLobster as a hospital would be to relax valid health and hygiene standards. But often, saying "no" is a way to avoid having to do something a little out of the ordinary that could as easily be done. And much to the customer's delight.

If you're saying "no" often and about the same requests time and again, maybe you're overlooking a potentially profitable new line of business. Saying "yes" is what satisfies customers and convinces them you're in business to meet their needs.

20

Don't Leave Customers Hanging

Doing business with a business today often means working with multiple levels in a company. Each new contact is a journey through a new and unfamiliar maze of people and systems. Customers can get lost in the process. And if they can't find their way through your systems and people to a satisfying conclusion, they won't come back.

When customers need directions to another department, don't just point the way — take them there yourself. Similarly, don't transfer customer phone calls blindly. Instead, tell them where they're being transferred and why, then stay on the line to make sure the connection is made. By taking the extra moment or two to play tour guide, you're transforming a strange business landscape into a familiar one customers will enjoy visiting again.

STRATEGY 3:
MANAGE THE FIRST IMPRESSIONS

Everything counts for the customer. Everything.

21. Conduct A Dawn Patrol

22. Make Personal Contact

23. Make The Customer Feel Important

24. Be Helpful — And Patient

25. Clean Up Your Act

26. Give Tangible Quality Clues

27. Be Personally Accessible

28. Offer Guarantees

29. Offer Contingencies

30. Play Fair With Your Customer

21

Conduct A Dawn Patrol

Before you open your doors to your customers, check over your facilities. In the late night and early morning hours, or over the weekend, things can come unraveled without anyone noticing. You don't want your customer to be the first one to point out that the cleaning service dumped a day's worth of trash in the bushes or local street artists decorated your walls. Getting each new business day off to a positive start can have benefits all day long.

The Dawn Patrol is equally effective with people. Don't skulk in your office with a cup of coffee and a dour demeanor. Let your people know that it's a new day and you're ready for whatever it brings. And since, as Will Rogers once noted, "people learn more from observation than conversation," the fact that you consider it important enough to start your day out front won't be lost on your people.

Customers consistently value four things in the service providers they choose to do business with: personal attention, dependability, promptness and employee competence. A sincere and professional greeting acknowledging that you're aware of them and welcome their business scores points on all four.

Everyone in your organization should be trained to greet customers personally and personably. Face-to-face, emphasize eye contact, body language and a visible willingness to serve. Over the phone, make sure your people identify both themselves and the business by name — and offer service. Help customers connect personally with your people by providing name tags, business cards, desk plates and other professional courtesies.

22

Make Personal Contact

23

Make The Customer Feel Important

People go back to places they enjoy, to businesses that make them feel individually important and cared for, where they feel they receive good value for their money. Show respect, courtesy and caring to all customers at all times. Above all, listen to them: They'll tell you what they want and how they want it, which helps you figure out how to satisfy them.

Good service is both obvious and subtle. In some Dun & Bradstreet locations, they've thrown away their "Visitor" badges (rationale: a visitor is an outsider, someone who doesn't belong and has to be watched carefully). Now when guests sign in, they receive a badge that says "Customer." That way, everyone who meets them can recognize them for the VIPs they truly are.

Customers will never understand your business the way you do. They don't always know exactly what they want or which person or department can best help them. Often they're nervous or insecure about approaching a total stranger to ask for assistance. How your people respond speaks volumes about the kind of business they work for.

If a particular employee isn't in, don't just take a message. Instead, teach your people to introduce themselves by name and offer to help the customer or direct them to someone else who can be of assistance. In Ritz Carlton hotels, employees at every level are taught that anyone who hears a problem, question or complaint "owns" it until it is resolved. At Southern Bell, "a promise to a customer by an employee commits all employees to help fulfill it."

24

Be Helpful — And Patient

25

Clean Up Your Act

The first impression your customers have on arriving at your place of business isn't the person who greets them as they walk in. It's everything they see, hear, walk around, step over or duck under between wherever they have to park and your front door. The cleanliness and accessibility of your buildings, landscaping and signage, the exterior and interior layout, even signs making it clear who has privileged parking spaces in your lot all communicate a message to your customers. McDonald's tells its crew kids, "If you've got time to lean, you've got time to clean."

Here's how SuperAmerica, a regional gas-and-goods chain, defines the proper level of detail: "From the customer's point of view, if they can see it, walk on it, hold it, hear it, step in it, smell it, step over it, touch it, use it, even taste it, if they can feel it or sense it, it's customer service."

26

Give Tangible Quality Clues

Service is produced and delivered simultaneously, which means customers' observations of the process will greatly influence their judgment of the quality of your products and services. Former airline executive Donald Burr once observed that when the little flipdown tray on the back of the airplane seat in front of you won't lock in place or is coffee-stained, the passenger's first thought is, "I wonder how good they are at engine maintenance."

Your marketing and sales literature, logo and letterhead, anything customers can get their hands around, provide tangible clues to the quality of your services. They had better be as good as you are. Develop a consistent "family" look that says your business is being run by design, not blind random chance. If you cut corners on your own quality, why should customers think you won't cut corners on them?

27

Be Personally Accessible

Give long-term or key customers access to you during business hours through a direct line. After hours, make sure they have your home phone number (if personal privacy is a consideration, add a separate listing and put a recorder on it so you can get the message without disrupting family time).

The value of having a direct number is lost if callers still have to negotiate their way past an officious secretary or gatekeeper. The filtering process also deprives you of direct feedback from your customers. Executives of Amdahl, a computer manufacturer in California's Silicon Valley, often pop into the lobby unannounced to talk to customers. Top executives from Stew Leonard (from Stew Leonard's renowned Connecticut dairy store) to First Wachovia Bank president John G. Medlin Jr. answer their own phones and mail.

Know your business well enough to know what things you can do on a consistent and reliable basis. Then back them up with specific guarantees so your customers know you're serious about your service quality. But a word of caution: Make your guarantees straightforward and unconditional — like Domino's 30 minutes or Federal Express' "absolutely, positively" — because customers won't believe them if they come with lots of clauses and exceptions.

Deluxe Corporation prints about half the checks used by both businesses and households. It promises 48-hour turnaround on all orders and zero defects — every order will be right the first time. It knows from experience that, 99-point-something times out of 100, that's a commitment it can and will meet. And it works very hard to eliminate the rare exceptions.

28

Offer Guarantees

29

Offer Contingencies

Not everything that affects the customer's experience with your product or service is within your control. You can't promise your customers sunny weather, but you can promise to hold an umbrella over them when it rains. The point is to make them want to come back and do business with you again, not enforce the strict letter of a rule or policy.

Perceptive service providers understand that sometimes the flight is late, or the babysitter didn't show up, or the phone rang at the wrong time, and look for a way to salvage the experience for the customer as well as for themselves. The legendary service manual at Nordstrom is eloquently simple: "Use your good judgment in all situations," it advises, adding, "There will be no additional rules."

The key to building a lasting relationship with customers is to see them as vital parts of your business' long-term success, not convenient sources of immediate cashflow. Hustling them for an extra dollar now won't pay off in the long run. Neither will the hallowed mushroom treatment: keeping them in the dark and feeding them a steady diet of bullshit.

Car dealers are notorious for offering hot dogs and balloons and all kinds of glad-handing, then structuring the deal with so many blind alleys and hidden costs that you leave feeling like you've been had. As a result, most Americans go to a different car dealer to buy their next car. On the other hand, companies such as Digital Equipment (DEC) pride themselves in talking their customers down to lower-priced products if that will meet their needs.

30

Play Fair With Your Customer

STRATEGY 4:
MANAGE THE DETAILS

There are no silver bullets. The key to superior service quality is not to get 100% better at any one thing, but rather to get one percent better at a hundred different things ... and then do it all over again.

31. See The Trees

32. Create Valid Expectations

33. Expect The Best From Your Business

34. Coordinate Your Services

35. Educate Customers — And Potential Customers

36. Be Honest With Your Customers

37. Don't Over-Promise

38. Take Returns And Exchanges

39. Resist "Acceptable Quality Levels"

40. Anticipate *Your* Tomorrow

31

See The Trees

Jan Carlzon, the architect of SAS' legendary service transformation, explains that in its customer's eyes, "SAS exists a *moment of truth* at a time." He defines a moment of truth as any time the customer comes in contact with the organization and has a chance to judge the quality of its services. SAS, he maintains, has 50,000 moments of truth *a day* — every one of which has to be managed to come out in the customer's favor.

Centralization can leave you focused only on the forest. Compare that to the time-honored watchword of retailing: "Retail is detail." Don't lose your close-to-the-customer perspective in favor of broad averages and norms. Try to see your business as customers see it, one tree, one transaction, one moment of truth at a time. You don't improve service quality in general. You do it *in specific*.

Many businesses overlook the fact that what their customers expect from them has a lot to do with the expectations the business itself creates. Customers have to learn how to be customers. They have to find out how you differ from your competitors. They have to discover when they're supposed to be satisfied. Smart businesses teach them by managing their expectations and their experiences toward well-defined (and customer-biased) service quality standards.

If you say you'll return the call by the end of the day, do so; if you can't, give the customer a different deadline. If you promise the order by noon, deliver by noon; if you aren't sure whether you can, don't make the promise. If your sign says you open at 8, don't unlock the doors at 8:25; if you can't open until 8:30, put that on the sign.

32

Create Valid Expectations

33

Expect The Best From Your Business

Treat your business as a stage where a people-pleasing performance has to take place time after time. The set has to be right. The lighting has to be right. The actors have to know their lines. The seats have to be clean and comfortable.

Disney has built one of the world's most admired businesses on essentially the same entertainment experience you can get at any State Fair. The difference they call *imagineering*: managing everything the customer (or "guest," in their vernacular) sees, hears, feels and experiences. From top management to the people who sweep the streets or climb inside the character costumes, every "cast member" (which is what Disney calls its employees) is expected to carry on the traditions and high service standards of the organization. Every day.

Accuracy and timely access to records, bills and customer files are important contributors to the level of trust the customer has in you. But the impact of fast, attentive service in one department will be lost if the customer ends up waiting 45 minutes somewhere else. And extra hours will lose their impact if essential support services are only available during "normal" hours. Systems need to work together, not against each other.

Manage the entire process, not just the individual stages. Cross-reference purchase and warranty records. Make sure customers aren't being dunned for late payment on a bill for something they returned six weeks ago. If frontline people who need access to customer or business data can't get it quickly and efficiently, your customer will begin wondering how you're managing to stay in business.

34

Coordinate Your Services

35

Educate Customers — And Potential Customers

You know more about your business than your customer does. Sharing that knowledge can actually help things run smoother. If your service is new or unfamiliar, help customers learn more about it. As they find ways to use your products and services to their fullest potential, you increase the value you provide them *and* the business they provide you.

Quad/Graphics, an innovative Wisconsin-based printing company, keeps customers abreast of fast-changing technology by sponsoring "camps" at which customers learn first-hand how to get best value for their printing dollars. H&R Block prospects for new tax preparers by offering classes to the general public. Home Depot home-improvement centers and Williams-Sonoma kitchen stores both win kudos for showing customers how to use the things they sell.

There's a natural tendency to try to put the best face on things, delaying or disguising unpleasant tasks rather than tackling them head-on. But that only compounds customer dissatisfaction. When delivery dates change, problems occur, promises — explicit or implied — are broken, inform your customers as soon as possible. They should hear both the good news and the bad news direct. Left to their own imagination, people will always imagine the worst.

The airlines have systematically changed flight schedules in recent years, adding a few extra minutes between published departure and arrival times to account for delays everyone knows are inherent in the system. As a result, "on time" arrivals are up. And customers are actually happier because they know what time they'll really be getting somewhere.

36

Be Honest With Your Customers

37

Don't Over-Promise

In the rush to try to be all things to all customers, many businesses stretch the limits of what they can do in a consistent and reliable manner. But service doesn't end at the sale, it begins. Get the relationship off on the right foot and it has a chance to develop into a long and happy journey.

Airline passengers don't care whether the plane lands at 10:12 or 10:15. They do care if it lands at *12:15* and they miss their connection. Splitting hairs over inconsequential details takes valuable time and attention away from matters of greater consequence. It also says you don't have a realistic idea of what your customer really wants. Customers take their cue from you — their expectations are based on what you've led them to expect. Be realistic. Disappointed and disgruntled customers will go somewhere else the next time.

There's no better way to turn a negative into a positive than by quickly and cheerfully processing a return or exchange. Sometimes customers buy the wrong size, or three too many of the right one, or change their minds when they get it home. Make them feel valued and they'll buy from you again. Treat them like petty criminals and they'll find someone else to do business with in the future.

From mail-order leaders L.L. Bean and Lands' End to Nordstrom and other customer-focused retailers, the best return policies are simple and nonconfrontive: "You bought it. You don't like it. We'll take it back. Period." Yes, there are dishonest people out there. Statistically speaking, they are few in number and proportion. The question you have to answer is whether you want to treat your good customers like potential crooks or your occasional misfits like potential good customers.

38

Take Returns And Exchanges

39

Resist 'Acceptable Quality Levels'

Nobody's perfect. Nobody can be perfect. It's easy to rationalize a certain "acceptable" level of substandard performance. But it's a trap to avoid because it too often becomes a self-fulfilling prophecy. Accept the idea that 15% of your customers will quit you in a huff each year and you'll likely discover at least that many do so. After all, you've let everyone in the organization know that's "normal."

To attain "zero defections" among customers, set "zero defects" as the standard of performance in dealing with them. That means the only acceptable quality level is 100%. If you doubt that, ask yourself whether 90%, or 95%, or even 99% would be an acceptable quality level for landing airplanes or picking up babies in a hospital nursery. Isn't what you're doing equally important?

Will Rogers once wrote, "Even if you're on the right track, if you're not moving, the train runs over you." How will your business be affected if export markets open up for your product or service? Can your computer system be connected to data retrieval and network services? Will you be able to meet your customers' needs if they go to 24-hour operations or decentralize their management or purchasing functions?

Investigate and plan for future customer needs and expectations so that you will be ready and able to meet — and exceed — them instead of being forced to react and play catch-up while a competitor gains ground at your expense. Select systems and equipment that can grow and change as your business does. Prepare people for future challenges through cross-training and other lifelong development activities.

40

Anticipate
Your
Tomorrow

STRATEGY 5:
SOLVE PROBLEMS

Research shows that at any given time, about one fourth of the customers of a typical business are dissatisfied enough to start doing business with someone else (if they can find someone else — and in today's global service economy, they usually can). To bring the customer back when things go wrong is one of the most productive investments you can make.

41. Plan For Service Breakdowns

42. Blame The Performance, Not The People

43. Be Honest With Your Employees

44. Cut The Red Tape

45. Involve Customers In Solutions

46. Handle Problems Where They Occur

47. Don't Just Buy Peace And Quiet — Fix The System

48. Apologize

49. Make Atonement

50. Recapture Customer Loyalty

41

Plan For Service Breakdowns

Manufacturing processes have multiple levels of quality control to spot product that doesn't meet spec or fix things that break down. On the service side, however, there's seldom a corresponding recognition that the system won't always function perfectly. When it doesn't, customers and employees alike are unpleasantly surprised — and often frustrated because there's no clear system to handle the problem. Even when the company is perfect, research shows that about 30% of all business problems are caused by the customer — the idea that the customer is always right is wrong!

Give your employees tools and techniques for dealing with service breakdowns. For recurring problems, establish guidelines based on what your customers expect you to do to make things right. Take the initiative. Damage control is a poor way to build customer loyalty.

Managers need to be able to separate their people from what they do if they're to create a true problem-solving climate. They need to become adept at delivering constructive criticism that leads to improved performance without destroying the individual's self-esteem and motivation. Otherwise, employees afraid of being held personally responsible for a service snafu will work to cover up the problem rather than report or resolve it.

Empowerment means making employees personally responsible for customer satisfaction. If it doesn't come out right the first time, they need to know that you expect them to stay with the problem until it's settled. The manager's role is a service one. As Domino's expresses it, "If you don't make it, bake it or take it, then you're support for those who do."

42

Blame The Performance, Not The People

43

**Be Honest
With Your
Employees**

Internal customers are every bit as important to your organization's external success as the customers who purchase your goods or services. The same standards of performance and problem-solving apply to them too. When you break a promise — explicit or implied — to an employee, admit it. Employees will respect your honesty — and learn from your example.

Tom Peters notes that employees study their managers as a basic survival practice. If they observe that the only service that counts to you is lip service, that's what they'll provide. If you alibi your way out of the periodic service problem, or manipulate standards for your own comfort and convenience, they'll apply the same practice to their own mix-ups with customers. Honesty really is the best policy.

Customers don't like to fill out forms, make multiple phone calls and write letters to have problems fixed, especially when they think — as they're prone to do — that you caused the problem. Of the 25 out of 100 customers who statistically speaking are dissatisfied, only *one* will ever complain. The rest will suffer in silence (and beat feet to a competitor) rather than put themselves through the ordeal of trying to get satisfaction out of an adversarial and cumbersome system that often makes them feel they're at fault.

Too often, rules are simply policies that harden with time. Originally created to provide a convenient system for getting work done, they can take on a life of their own and ultimately get in the way of the work — serving and satisfying the customer. To get yourself back in the customer's good graces, first fix the customer. Then take care of the forms.

44

Cut The Red Tape

45

Involve Customers In Solutions

It's easy to assume you know what the problem is and how it should be resolved. On the other hand, don't forget the cynical formula that says, "To ass/u/me always makes an a—" ... you know the rest. Customers expect to be listened to and they want the response to the problem they report to be appropriate to their needs, not mindlessly selected from a checklist or catalog. Customers who complain and are responded to can actually become *more loyal* than those who pronounce themselves satisfied.

One size seldom fits all. Instead of reacting on reflex, ask customers how they would like the situation resolved. Often their expectations will be simpler and more reasonable than your worst-guess scenarios. What's more, by involving them in problem resolution, you're involving them in putting the relationship back in order.

If your people can be present at the creation of a service problem, why should they not be involved in its resolution? Whenever possible, don't shuffle customers off to an isolated claims or complaint department (even if it does have the misleading designation of "Customer Service"). Train people throughout the organization so they're prepared to provide prompt and effective redress when, or soon after, a problem occurs.

First Wachovia, a regional bank holding company serving the Southeast, is one of many that adheres to "the Sunset Rule" — never let the sun set on a problem without first reporting its status to the customer. That doesn't mean it promises to fix things in less than 24 hours. It means that before the end of the business day, the customer hears from someone who can report status and when action can be expected.

46

Handle Problems Where They Occur

47

Don't Just Buy Peace And Quiet — Fix The System

Complaining customers can be a true asset to the business if you're paying attention. A complaining customer has decided there's still something in the relationship worth saving — otherwise, why complain? Research suggests that for every disgruntled customer, there may be 24 more who have had similar experiences but won't tell you about them. (On average, however, they will tell 14 to 20 people about what they didn't like).

Consistent or repeated complaint patterns can help you identify parts of your business that are not functioning smoothly. Ask your customers to critique your systems for promptness and dependability, your documentation for clarity and accuracy. Use their feedback to revise, streamline and improve performance. Track customer complaints and problems, then use that information to correct systemic faults.

Too often, businesses fall into an "us against them" attitude when it comes to problem solving. The kind of foolish, stiff-necked pride that resists taking responsibility for an incident that turned out wrong — no matter whose fault it might have been — can alienate even very loyal customers. It also teaches employees to be defensive, unreceptive to complaints, even arrogant in their treatment of customers.

Research shows that more than anything else, customers expect an apology and a prompt response when something goes wrong. That alone may be enough to persuade them to give you another chance. If the customer's future business really is important to you, apologize for the inconvenience suffered. Whether or not you caused the problem, it costs you nothing, and it gives evidence of your desire to restore a valued relationship.

48

Apologize

49

Make Atonement

When appropriate, compensate a customer for the problem — before anyone starts talking about a lawyer. If the problem was minor, the atonement may be symbolic: a simple gesture that says, "We would like to make it up to you." If major, a more substantial response may be in order. Hardee's teaches even teenaged fast-food workers, "Don't Fight, Make It Right." Marriott hotels have well-planned response procedures for those occasions when problems occur.

If it costs five times as much money to attract a new customer as it does to retain one you already have, what's at stake is a relationship that it's generally in your financial interest to continue. Isn't it worth a few dollars off, or a one-time free ride, to keep a customer who may do business with you for years to come?

Generally speaking, there's only about a one-in-three chance that customers who are dissatisfied but don't complain to you about it will do business with you again — about one-in-10 if the value of the transaction in question was greater than $100. But customers who complain and are responded to, even if the response doesn't come out in their favor, tend to come back as much as 95% of the time.

Like any other productive relationship, both parties have a mutual interest in continuing an association based on past satisfaction and trust. Don't let a problem fester. Work not only to resolve the cause of the complaint but to regain the goodwill and loyalty of the customer. Following through after the problem has been handled reminds your customers that you continue to value their business.

50

Recapture Customer Loyalty

STRATEGY 6:
EVALUATE TREATMENT OF CUSTOMERS

*Service is delivered one-on-one, a fleeting interaction
between a customer and a frontline worker. To
manage service well, those transactions must be
constantly sampled and evaluated.*

51. Phone Home

52. Survey Customers

53. Acknowledge Customer Comments With
    Enthusiasm

54. Survey Key Influences

55. Hire A Shopping Service

56. Enlist Your Customers In Mystery Shops

57. Share The Wealth Internally

58. Review Outgoing Customer Correspondence

59. Evaluate Billing Systems

60. Give Customers The Benefit Of The Doubt

51

Phone Home

How do your customers encounter your business? Customers often have a very different impression of a business than the people who work within its walls. To experience your business from your customers' vantage point, go away. Then call in and, without identifying yourself, see how long it takes you to work your way through the complexities of the phone system, get answers to a question, help with a problem, access to a key individual.

When you call your own organization, is your firm's name clearly stated? Is the tone professional? Are you quickly connected to the right party? Or left on hold for minutes on end? Many AAA clubs now limit holds to no more than one minute and calls to no more than one transfer. If they can't do what needs to be done within those limits, they take the time necessary to get their act together and call back.

By phone, mail, point of contact cards, face-to-face interview or a combination of all of the above, seek constant feedback on how well your business is meeting customer needs and expectations. Ask specifically about products, service, delivery and support — and listen for the comments that don't fit the neat checklist boxes but tell you volumes. Look for ways to improve existing services and clues for meeting emerging needs.

Each Marriott hotel is expected to generate a specific number of after-stay comment cards. Embassy Suites hotel managers periodically buttonhole five guests a day for a week or two to get a reading on how they're enjoying their stay. Patient reps and nurses at Riverside Methodist Hospitals in Columbus, Ohio, annually make thousands of follow-up calls after discharge to see how their former patients are doing — and how Riverside did.

52

Survey Customers

53

Acknowledge Customer Comments With Enthusiasm

Make it easy for your customers to tell you how they feel by offering postage-paid bounce-back cards that solicit both specific and general information about their most recent experience with you. Some people won't or can't tell you what they're really thinking if you ask them face-to-face, but will use the less confrontive comment card to tell you about the service they received.

When customers call or write, whether to complain or compliment, acknowledge them with a letter or note. Do it sooner rather than later. Thank them for taking the time to help you serve them better. Let them know that you pay attention to customer feedback. At Stew Leonard's Dairy Store in Norwalk, CT, every suggestion dropped in the big box by the front door (100 a day is average) is personally acknowledged, in writing, within 48 hours.

Business-to-business relationships are seldom "one deep." Query purchasing agents, customer staff support people, the vendors in your distribution and supply chain, and anyone else who influences the continued use of your products or services.

Dataserv, a third-party computer maintenance firm, regularly surveys customers at multiple levels — executive, line, administrative — then cross-references the findings to make sure its people know whether customers are satisfied, services understood, problems solved, needs met.

Remember that information exchange is a two-way street. The feedback you give them helps them use your services better, just as the feedback they give you can help your people adjust their efforts. Use what you hear to tell people what they're doing *right* (so they'll keep doing it) as well as where you'd like to see improvement.

54

Survey Key Influences

55

Hire A Shopping Service

A third-party shopping firm can help you measure how well a typical transaction meets your customer service standards. "Secret shoppers" blend in with your normal customers, but they're specially trained to look for specific techniques and general practices that satisfy or frustrate.

Use the information they develop for you positively, not punitively. The point isn't to catch your people doing something wrong. It's to evaluate *from the customer's point of view* so you can fine-tune what you're doing and how you're doing it. According to Carol Cherry, president of Shop'n Chek, the nation's largest shopping service, many businesses use her company's services to catch employees doing something right so they can be rewarded for modeling good service behaviors.

Who knows better than your regular, loyal customers whether your products and services are truly satisfactory? Take advantage of their expertise as expert customers to monitor and improve service levels by asking frequent customers to "shop" you periodically and report back on their experience.

Every Domino's Pizza location has two mystery shoppers: real families whose identities are known only to corporate headquarters. Once a month, they place normal, everyday orders. Then they fill out an evaluation form that tracks 22 different variables, from how long the delivery took and how hot the pizza was to whether Domino's people are in uniform, courteous and driving safely. Their reports give each location a constant reading on its service and provide comparative benchmarks for others in the system.

56

**Enlist Your
Customers
In Mystery
Shops**

57

Share The Wealth Internally

The best survey in the world won't do your business any good unless and until you share the information with people throughout your organization. Making them smart about your business makes them better able to meet and exceed their customers' needs.

When Embassy Suites managers survey guests under their roof, they post the results *the next day* in all employee staff areas so everyone from housekeeping to the front desk knows how customers are responding. The 100 suggestions received daily at Stew Leonard's Dairy Store are typed up by 10 a.m. the following morning and distributed to all managers, with extra copies placed in employee break areas. Wal-Mart associates, regardless of their experience or salary level, receive constant updates on their store's performance compared to regional and national standards.

Evaluate the materials you send to customers — not only personal letters, but obvious form letters, bills and account statements, product literature, advertising and other public information. Are they easy to read and understand? Do they serve a useful purpose? Do they reinforce your willingness to serve, or will they confuse or irritate?

American Airlines uses its annual reports as primers on its operations so shareholders (an important class of customers) will understand how its business works. AMP consolidated 22 different engineering change systems to one so customers could more easily understand updates and modifications. A.G. Edwards & Sons, a regional brokerage firm, retooled its computer system to produce reformatted account statements that its customers could understand better. Every piece of mail is marketing literature. Make sure it represents you well.

58

Review Outgoing Customer Correspondence

59

Evaluate Billing Systems

How are your billing statements worded? Are they clear or confusing? Professional or threatening? Do they provide a means for customers to request clarification or assistance? Years of customer loyalty can be lost if the billing system isn't functioning smoothly. While more than one business has alienated customers when backlogged payment processing caused them to receive past-due bills, many also have impressed customers by spotting an aberration that indicates unauthorized activity on the account.

Don't overlook the opportunity to say thanks to customers who regularly pay on time. They'll be impressed you noticed. Customers of Midwest Delivery, a metro package service in Minneapolis/St. Paul, occasionally receive an invoice in a special envelope with gold-foil stickers inside and out to thank them for keeping accounts current.

Too many businesses operate in problem/solution mode, seeing every new situation as a problem that must be resolved by immediate and forceful action on their part. Sometimes what looks like a problem isn't ... until you make it one.

Customers deserve — and expect — the benefit of the doubt. Don't polarize them or push them into the waiting arms of your competitors by treating them in adversarial ways. Listen with an open mind. Then respond as appropriate. Or enlist an objective third party to help resolve disagreements — the American Automobile Association now provides arbitration service for some automobile companies' independent dealers and will referee problems between members and repair shops participating in its Approved Auto Repair program.

60

Give Customers The Benefit Of The Doubt

STRATEGY 7:
EVALUATE TREATMENT AT THE FRONTLINE

Take care of your employees and they'll take care of your customers.

61. View Employees As Internal Customers

62. Be A Service Role Model

63. Remove Barriers

64. Communicate Internally

65. Compare Internal And External Measures

66. Pay For Performance

67. Promote Wisely

68. Allocate Perks For Service

69. Develop Service-Focused Managers

70. Avoid "Seagull Management"

61

View Employees As Internal Customers

At Scandinavian Airlines System (SAS), the rule of thumb is: If you're not serving a customer, your job is to be serving someone who is. They believe and act on the premise that they have two kinds of people: Customer service people and "other." Management is "other." It's also the most crucial service in today's business organization. And employees are its primary customers.

Managers who use power and authority negatively often are afraid to turn their backs on their people — and with good reason. How *you* treat your people has a direct impact on how *they* treat your customers. As it says in the Walt Disney World handbook: Guests (customers) will receive the treatment they should receive from cast members (employees) when cast members receive that same kind of treatment from their managers.

No matter what kind of business you're in, the people around you don't accept what you say at face value. They watch what you do for clues to your real priorities and concerns. If the boss dodges unpleasant duties, leaves customers on hold, communicates poorly or not at all, or otherwise shrugs off customer concerns, employees will do the same. Soon, customers will notice that the only kind of service they're getting is lip service. In no time at all, they'll be someone else's customers.

Service is an area where managers need to lead by example. At Bergen Brunswig, a pharmaceutical wholesaler, top executives make up to 100 sales calls a year. Wal-Mart sends its headquarters staffers into the stores for at least one week each year so they remember their roots. The frontlines are where the action is. Visit them regularly.

62

Be A Service Role Model

63

**Remove
Barriers**

Too many businesses stubbornly refuse to dismantle outmoded systems, policies and procedures that exist primarily for the convenience of internal managers — and that, over time, come to work at cross purposes with doing things to satisfy customers. If you ignore customers or make it harder than it has to be to do business with you, they will indeed go away.

Ask employees what things impede the delivery of distinctive service. Then involve them in finding ways to work around or dismantle the barriers so the business functions even more smoothly. In recent years, employees at every level of American Airlines have contributed some 2,000 ideas for improving the way the company does business, resulting in more than $20 million in cost savings and new revenues ... and improved customer service ratings as well.

Your people work with your systems and your customers on a day-to-day basis. They have functional knowledge of what works and what doesn't — knowledge that can make your business run smoother and be more competitive. But very few managers ever ask them for their ideas, experiences, observations and suggestions. Consequently, and contrary to popular belief, most employees don't *burn out* — they *rust out* from being used at less than their full potential.

Research shows that a strong service culture starts from the top with involved management that is committed to service quality and accessible to people throughout the organization. Don't overlook one of your most powerful resources. Ask employees to assess how well current management practices support them in providing high quality customer service. Then act on what you hear.

64

Communicate Internally

65

Compare Internal And External Measures

There is a strong correlation between how well employees believe they are being managed and how well customers believe they are being served. The two are very closely related. You can't provide good service to customers if your people aren't selected and trained properly and service systems are dysfunctional, but you also won't meet service quality targets if your people are poorly managed or company systems and policies get in the way of their best efforts.

While you work to find multiple ways to get close to your external customers, you can achieve equally strong results from making sure internal customers in your organization are being properly served. Survey them formally. Talk to them informally — and frequently. Encourage their suggestions. Involve them in task forces and work teams that have real-world objectives and responsibilities.

66

Pay For Performance

Just as it costs five times as much to attract a new customer as it does to retain one you already have, there are very real pay-offs in keeping experienced performers in your organization. Yet many businesses continue to watch their best people leave to work for better-paying competitors — losing valuable knowledge and experience where it's needed most, at the frontlines, plus writing off every dollar invested in training and managing that individual, *plus* incurring the cost of finding and training a replacement.

You get what you pay for. Stew Leonard's recruits customer-pleasing cashiers in part because it pays a little bit more than the other places where those cashiers could work. Nordstrom salespeople can earn more than $50,000 a year on the sales floor, Federal Express and UPS drivers upwards of $30,000 making deliveries.

67

Promote Wisely

One of the age-old traps of structured organizations is promoting top performers to supervisory positions simply because they're top performers. In an instant, you've lost a star at the frontlines and gained a supervisor who may have neither the skills nor the inclination to manage other people effectively.

A "dual career track" helps you reward good people while keeping them in positions where they can continue to succeed for your customers. At 3M, scientists and researchers who provide the impetus for new offerings can move up to product management positions — or they can stay in the lab and work on more new products. Either way, their careers continue to advance. When you do move someone up, make sure you're rewarding service skills and performance, not just doing business "by the numbers."

At Beyer Volvo in Falls Church, VA, the best mechanic in the shop each month earns the use of a $40,000 showroom special for the next 30 days. Drivers for SuperShuttle, an airport van service based in Los Angeles, can earn paid days off based on the number of passengers they've carried in the preceding month. Pacesetting sales associates in Nordstrom stores get a 33% discount on their purchases compared to the 20% offered to everyone else who works there.

Every business has — or can develop — highly visible perks that can motivate and reward service achievements: reserved parking spaces, tickets to special events, discounts and privileges. Traditionally they've been used with managers, but they work as well at the frontline. The tactic will only be effective, however, if those perks go (with as little delay as possible) to the people who do the work that earns them.

68

Allocate Perks For Service

69

Develop Service-Focused Managers

If management is the ultimate service within the organization, it follows that managers need to learn how to serve effectively. In many top service organizations, the emphasis today is on coaching skills: learning how to work with individuals to build them into members of skilled, high-performing, motivated teams that focus on service quality.

One of the best places to train managers is the frontlines. Procter & Gamble's management cadre all started in frontline jobs. So did more than half of Disney's. H&R Block offices are managed by people who have come up through the ranks, while Domino's franchises are offered only to store managers (most of whom started as frontline workers) who have demonstrated their service skills as well as their potential for running a business.

70

Avoid 'Seagull Management'

Author Ken Blanchard notes that seagulls are graceful, imposing birds ... from a distance. Up close, they're rude, crude and obnoxious — scavengers that feed in garbage dumps and leave their mark all over everything. Too many managers have learned to operate the same way, swooping down on hapless employees, picking up a few scraps, squawking at them, dumping on them, then flying off and leaving them to clean up the mess.

Managers need to use information to build up, not tear down performers. When research identifies a shortfall, the appropriate response is to build performance back toward target levels, not pounce on the people who might appear to be responsible. United Parcel Service uses the concept of "least best" — never singling out just one individual for attention, but working with a number of people to improve group performance.

STRATEGY 8:
DEVELOP YOUR PEOPLE

Customers consistently define satisfying service as a combination of personal attention, dependability, promptness and employee competence. In simplest terms, your business is as good as your people.

71. Expect The Best From Your People

72. Select Based On Customer Contact Needs

73. Staff Smart

74. Train And Educate

75. Empower

76. Cross-Train And Cross-Sell

77. Give Credit Where Credit Is Due

78. Reward And Celebrate

79. Post Letters Of Praise

80. Provide Management Support

71

Expect The Best From Your People

Disney has built one of the world's most admired businesses with a workforce composed primarily of teenagers and young adults — the same kids you can't get to close the refrigerator or pick up their socks at home operate and maintain multi-million-dollar entertainment complexes. No one at Disney (or Federal Express, or L.L. Bean, or any other outstanding service exemplar) accepts the shopworn alibi, "You just can't get good help these days." They know different.

And they expect different. Rather than be content with mediocre performance, they set exceptionally high standards, and then manage to achieve them. Every Disney employee, regardless of job description, is considered a "cast member." They're all in the show. And the system works because Disney selects well, trains in-depth and then expects all employees to perform to the best of their abilities.

Not everyone belongs in customer contact. A level of stress, tension and pressure to perform to meet the constantly changing needs and expectations of fickle customers is necessarily built into frontline jobs. Superior service requires analysis and communication skills some workers simply don't have — or want to have. Others positively thrive on the constant challenge and interpersonal interaction. Those are the ones you want.

Don't think you can "teach" people to smile, or be cheerful and courteous, or project an outside demeanor that isn't built on their own bedrock character. Look for those who relate well to others, who express themselves well and take visible personal pride in themselves and the work they do. Then give them the training they need to apply those traits to the needs of your customers.

72

Select Based On Customer Contact Needs

73

Staff Smart

Even the best service team will frazzle and self-destruct when stretched too thin or asked too often to be too many different things to too many different people. Manage your workforce to make sure you're staffed to meet slightly more than the anticipated level of customer demand. And build in several back-ups so you can respond smoothly to unforeseen situations.

Hospitals have learned that all patients do not have equal needs: They now use formulas that assign acuity ratings based on the amount of nursing care required to determine how much staff will be needed on a given shift. From fast food to department stores and high-tech firms, full-time employees are augmented with part-time, flextime, job-sharing and even on-call workers who can make sure that customers aren't left waiting — or sent elsewhere.

It's easy to identify the basic skills people need to meet the general requirements of their jobs. But it's equally important to make sure they know *why* they're doing what they're doing. And how well or poorly. Do your people know how the business works? Do they realize the impact of their actions — and inactions — on customer loyalty and the bottom line? Do they understand why they are supposed to do what they are supposed to do? They won't unless you tell them.

Share the reasons for your business strategy and the results of your management measures with employees. Make sure they know, first-hand, immediately, "warts and all," what their customers are saying in research, focus groups, comment cards and other measurements. Focus on things employees can impact. The smarter they are about *your* business, the better able they'll be to do *their* jobs.

74

Train And Educate

75

Empower

Empowerment is more than a new buzzword. It's a crucial tactical edge to give your employees. Research shows the more people involved in a transaction, the less likely the customer is to be satisfied. Customers want to deal with one person who can meet their needs, answer their questions, solve their problems and send them home happy. Empowered employees know customer satisfaction is their personal responsibility. What's more, they accept that responsibility and act on it.

Effective empowerment requires a thorough understanding of what customers need and expect, an in-depth knowledge of what the business can do for them, and access to the resources (including management involvement and support) needed to get the job done. Hire and train employees who can use their "own good judgment" — then let them.

You can help both your organization and your employees grow if you teach and involve people in more than their own narrow jobs. At Embassy Suites, employees can elect to be trained for jobs in other departments, even if there are no immediate openings. Until there are, they're paid a little extra for the extra skills they've acquired.

The practice not only helps develop long-term employees with multiple skills to offer, it also provides back-up capabilities for unpredictable staffing challenges. If the front desk is suddenly overwhelmed by a large number of arrivals, chances are there's someone in housekeeping or AV who can fill in through the rush. Similarly, Delta Air Lines flight crews know how to pitch in to help gate agents check their passengers through — which means they have a better chance to get their flight off on time, and with happier passengers aboard.

76

Cross-Train And Cross-Sell

77

Give Credit Where Credit Is Due

Sharing the spotlight builds morale internally as well as customer loyalty externally. No one can do it alone in business these days. Good salespeople are no better than the supporting personnel backing them up. Doctors depend on nurses, nurses on aides and orderlies. Airline flight crews would never get off the ground without mechanics, gate agents and baggage handlers who do their jobs right. All players on the service team need to be recognized for their contributions.

At Goldman Sachs, one of the most respected brokerage firms on Wall Street, members of project teams wrap up each job by writing "credit memos" that acknowledge who did what and why it was important. When employees are up for partnerships, those credit memos become important selection criteria: not just the ones in the individual's file, but also the ones the individual has written.

Superior service is a pattern of individual behavior that can be modeled and imitated by others. The trick is simple: What gets rewarded gets repeated. Pacesetting service companies such as Federal Express, American Express, Delta Air Lines, LensCrafters and Southern Bell all work hard — and regularly — to make service heroes of frontline workers who satisfy customers. They take time out, often on the spot, to make a point of who did what right so everybody can learn from the good example.

Publicly celebrate and tangibly reward good service performers. Hold them up as role models for others to follow. Make their stories part of your organization's folklore — the anecdotal evidence of how individuals rise to their specific service challenges. Use their leadership to blaze a trail for everyone else to follow.

78

Reward And Celebrate

79

Post Letters Of Praise

It's important to share customer compliments with employees — both the individual involved and others in the organization around them. Unsolicited, positive feedback provides powerful evidence that superior service is not only noticed by customers, but valued by them. And by the organization.

At L.L. Bean, customer correspondence is posted on a bulletin board under the heading, *Memos from the Boss.* LensCrafters associates who are mentioned by name in customer correspondence receive a special President's Pin; Citicorp employees so mentioned wear gold name tags instead of silver ones. Southern Bell's renowned "Count On Me" recognition program includes ways for customers — as well as managers and co-workers — to nominate employees who have served them well.

80

Provide Management Support

Treating employees as customers represents a significant change from authoritarian management styles. Managers accustomed to forting up in their offices and summoning the troops for an audience (or a dressing down) don't function well in the modern service economy, any more than a director can judge how well the play went from the number of ticket stubs on the floor the next morning.

You can't manage a performance in absentia. To monitor and fine-tune the processes and attitudes that combine to please the customer, managers have to be visible and positively involved in the service side of the business. In that context, abusive treatment doesn't work — your people simply pass it along. The way you treat them is the way they will treat customers. The "trickle down" theory works in customer service, too.

STRATEGY 9:
ENFOLD CUSTOMERS IN YOUR BUSINESS

If you want your customers to remain your customers, make them feel a part of your business. Make them partners in a long-term business relationship that benefits you both.

81. Interact With Customers

82. Use Names

83. Learn From Competitors — And Peers

84. Beta Test Your Offerings

85. Develop Partnerships

86. Create Customer Advisory Boards

87. Reward Your Good Customers

88. Celebrate Your Successes With Customers

89. Get Involved With Customers

90. Provide Public Service, Too

81

**Interact
With
Customers**

A relationship is a two-way interaction that has to be beneficial to both parties to continue. Focus on more than just winning your customers' business today. Listen to their comments and suggestions. Respond — personally — to their letters and phone calls. Resolve their problems and complaints. Help them serve their own customers better. Chances are, they'll help you invent your new products and services or refine your existing ones.

Electronics companies such as AMP and Digital Equipment rely on "early involvement" with customers to design new products and services and keep current offerings up to date. Retail leaders like Nordstrom rely on full-time sales associates because they're more likely to be on the floor the *next* time a customer comes back.

82

Use Names

If customers are individuals who must be satisfied one at a time, it follows that the "take a number, your turn automatically" approach to service can do more harm than good. Names are our culture's way of identifying each individual in specific, personal terms. Use them properly and productively.

Call your customers by name (good restaurants know that customers appreciate having their names pronounced correctly, too). Make a point of spelling names correctly in records and correspondence. Avoid getting too familiar too quickly: To be safe, use the last name at first, and a title if appropriate: "Thank you, Dr. Smith." Dr. Smith will let you know if she wants you to call her Lee. And teach your people to use their own names to let their customers know they have a personal stake in delivering satisfying service.

83

Learn From Competitors — And Peers

Few businesses will ever have 100% market share. Customer loyalties are transient and far from exclusive. That means your customers are also customers of your competition, and they're comparing your business to others with which they come in contact. Find out how you compare — and learn from the comparison.

Benchmarking is a technique used by many businesses to provide a standard of comparison for their own internal service assessments. It's also a way to learn from other businesses that are successfully facing similar challenges. Find a company in a noncompeting field that faces similar operational challenges: handling phone orders, making deliveries, staying open 24 hours a day. Then compare tactics and techniques that will make you both better.

Your customers can be sources of more than just revenue. As relationships grow, they take on new dimensions and provide new opportunities. If your customers benefit from doing business with you (there is, after all, cost in finding and qualifying new suppliers), they have a selfish interest in your continuing success. Look for ways to capitalize on that.

With the caveat that there should be mutual benefit, enlist customers to test new service offerings, brainstorm product or program modifications, give feedback on prototypes and pilot projects, identify future industry needs — even review new instructional material, advertising campaigns and promotional literature. They'll learn more about your commitment to serving them. You'll pick up tips on meeting their needs better.

84

Beta Test Your Offerings

85

Develop Partnerships

As businesses decentralize and specialize to serve niche markets and special interests, new opportunities arise constantly that may well be beyond the resources or outside the business strategy of the discoverer. That's not a problem if you're seeing your customers as potential allies in new business efforts.

When 3M scientists discovered a way to improve the recording performance of videotape, they faced a dilemma: 3M doesn't make VCRs, and no manufacturer had a system capable of using the new and improved media. Solution: 3M approached JVC, owner of the patents on VHS recording technology. Bingo. Super-VHS. Department stores stock Liz Claiborne clothing lines not only because the clothes are of high quality, but also because Claiborne supports them with display design, store fixtures, even employee training.

Think of them as a board of directors for (and from) the frontline. Not only can good customers provide knowledgeable input on what it takes to keep them satisfied, they also open up a channel of communication to the communities in which you operate. Make board membership more than window dressing — meet on a regular basis and commit yourself to learning from what you hear. Involve people from throughout your orgranization instead of restricting access to a handful of managers.

Don't overlook your critics. Pacesetting utility companies know the value of giving the consumerist gadflies who once dogged their every step a role in their advisory boards. Once inside the walls, their former adversaries not only gain a more realistic understanding of what the business has to do, they help the business do it in more satisfying ways.

86

**Create
Customer
Advisory
Boards**

87

Reward Your Good Customers

Use your computer systems and other programs to track frequent shoppers to learn what and when they buy. Then reward them for their purchases and long-term patronage. They'll value you all the more for knowing that you've noticed their continuing business. And you'll inspire the kind of word-of-mouth advertising that money never will be able to buy.

At Miller Business Systems, some office supply vendors have been known to cater lunches for wholesale account people who keep their products in stock and moving out to end-users. Car rental companies reward those who rent from them in high frequency by giving them a personal vehicle for their family to use for a year. Emerald People's Utility District, a public power company in Oregon, throws a summer picnic *for its customers*.

Celebrate Your Successes With Customers

After all, customers are the ones who made those successes possible in the first place. Remember: Long-term customers knew you "way back when." They can take justifiable pride in the knowledge that their business helped your business grow. Celebrating the good times with them reinforces the relationship you've been building over the years. And they'll be justifiably upset if they feel they've been used and discarded as no longer important.

You needn't endanger the next quarter's profits or disrupt operations. An occasional billboard, a congratulatory ad, even a couple dozen donuts or a bouquet of flowers is marketing money well spent for the goodwill it can create. It also sends a message to your own people: This is where our work goes. These are the people it's important to.

89

Get Involved With Customers

Professional firms in law, accounting, public relations and other fields not uncommonly expect their people to put in *pro bono* time with community and professional organizations. There's a customer relations aspect to such involvement. The same holds true with attending events and functions that are important to your customers, assisting at customer trade shows, sponsoring client information seminars and image advertising in trade publications. All work to make your customers feel you are in business together.

The reverse is equally valuable. Invite customers to your key industry events and trade shows if they can benefit from the information, contacts and exposure available. Ask them to provide seminars and training for your people or customers in noncompetitive fields. Be known "by the companies you keep."

People like to do business with businesses they admire and respect as responsible operations and good corporate citizens. They have little loyalty to businesses that make it clear their only interest in a market is maximizing short-term gain at the expense of long-term vitality. The best way to rub shoulders with your customers outside of business encounters is to play a responsible role in community affairs.

Drivers for SuperShuttle provide traffic reports for local radio stations. Arizona Public Service, a utility company, maintains a linguistics base made up of volunteer employees fluent in more than two dozen languages, and encourages people to ask its field service personnel for assistance whenever they're in need. AAA pioneered school safety patrols, handicapped driver equipment standards and driver's education.

90

Provide Public Service, Too

STRATEGY 10:
FOLLOW UP ... FOLLOW UP ... FOLLOW UP

Word-of-mouth advertising is still the most convincing kind. And nothing puts words in those mouths better than following through. It says the transaction just past was only the beginning of a long and, it is to be hoped, mutually beneficial relationship.

91. Conduct Project Reviews

92. Make Feedback A Given

93. Make Follow-Up Calls

94. Conduct Account Reviews

95. Keep Your Scheduled Commitments

96. Report Back To Customers Who Contact You

97. Contact Customers Who Complain

98. Contact Lost Customers

99. Contact Silent Customers

100. Say "Thank You"

91

**Conduct
Project
Reviews**

Just because the job got done, don't assume it was done to everyone's satisfaction. Whether it was a routine sale or one wrapped up in lots of special requests, review it now, while the details are still fresh in people's minds and impressions are still fluid. Doing so adds to both the specific account history and general store of knowledge available to you over the longer term.

Follow up each project or job to find out (1) whether your customer's expectations were met, (2) what your customer would like you to do differently the next time, and (3) what your customer would like you to do the same next time. Involve support people as well as those with direct customer contact. At the Battelle Memorial Institute, the world famous research lab, every project — whether it panned out or not — is evaluated in depth to make sure customer expectations were satisfied.

Over the years, too many customers learned from unpleasant experience that businesses didn't want to know about their dissatisfaction. That's why we all say "fine" when the waiter or waitress asks about the meal, even if it's anything but fine. Now that you want to know what they're experiencing, you need to find ways to encourage feedback.

Don't wait for your customer to initiate contact. After every sale, provide a postage-paid evaluation card that asks for a rating on service received — and service desired. Make sure there's a way for anonymous feedback, but encourage full disclosure. Information is much more valuable when you know its source and can mine for pertinent details. Then respond in turn. Acknowledge those who provide their name, and follow up with details on the resolution of the conditions they described.

92

Make Feedback A Given

93

**Make
Follow-Up
Calls**

A common complaint of customers who have bought cars and houses is that their salesperson or real estate broker promised to follow up to see how they liked their new purchase, but never was heard from again. After major sales, call on customers, in person or by phone, to assess satisfaction, check for problems and find out how you can help them in the future.

Longo Toyota, the pacesetting dealership in the Los Angeles area, follows up on every sale within 48 hours. Coldwell Banker real estate now trains and expects its brokers to stay involved with a buyer or seller for five full years after the sale, an attempt to build a relationship that can lead to referrals and more sales. United Van Lines retains a private research firm to survey 300 recent customers a month (except in November and December, in deference to holiday time constraints).

In many businesses, the rule of thumb is 80/20: 80% of sales come from about 20% of the customer base. Don't take the loyalty of your key accounts for granted. Make sure you're meeting the needs and expectations of these vitally important customers by knowing them in detail and constantly keeping up to date on their needs and experiences.

On a regular basis, sit down with the key customers who provide the majority of your sales and review the business you have done together during the period since the last review. Discuss the successful and disappointing aspects of each job or project, both from your company's point of view and from your customer's point of view. Then identify the specific actions that will lead to increased satisfaction between now and the next review. Be sure everyone on the account team knows what you've decided.

94

**Conduct
Account
Reviews**

95

Keep Your Scheduled Commitments

If you create an expectation with a customer, whether for the immediate future or the longer term, make sure you can and do keep it. Arrive for meetings a little ahead of time. Keep your appointments when they're scheduled — or let your customers know you're off schedule as soon as you realize that you may not be able to be punctual.

In government agencies in Montgomery County, Ohio (surrounding Dayton), everyone — from businesspeople seeking licenses and permits to welfare recipients coming in for counseling sessions — is expected to be seen within 15 minutes of their scheduled appointment time. County workers are also expected to personally confirm that they know someone is waiting for them and tell them how soon they'll be seen. The service promise is equally valid in the public sector and the private sector.

Communications is a back-and-forth process, much like a ping pong game. When the ball's in your court, you can't ignore it without losing points. And when you delay, your customers are wondering whether they should be looking for someone else to play with. Even if you're not the one who will be handling their request or problem, make sure they know you've handed them off to someone who's prepared to meet their needs.

If you make a promise to get back to someone by a given time, make sure you keep that promise — even if you can't give them all the information you hoped to have available. If there's no time element involved, create it: Set a deadline for yourself to make sure you follow through while the subject is still fresh in your customer's mind. Communicate the deadline to your customer, then keep it.

96

Report Back To Customers Who Contact You

97

Contact Customers Who Complain

Follow-up works whether you're reinforcing the loyalty of a satisfied customer or trying to earn a second chance with a disgruntled one. Relationships have their downs as well as ups. That's what makes them relationships. While some accounts are beyond salvage, many can be revived after the initial rancor has cooled.

For dissatisfied customers, breaking off a vendor relationship means they have to find someone new to do business with — and they know there's no guarantee they'll find better than what they had. They may welcome the opportunity to be welcomed back to the fold. What's more, research on the art of "recovery" — literally returning things to their previous satisfactory state — shows that follow-up is often the extra touch that tips the balance back in your favor.

Over time, some customers inevitably drop from the rolls and begin doing business elsewhere. Don't accept the status quo, especially if you're not sure why they left. Find out. If there was a problem, do your best to rectify it. Invite them to keep you in mind as their needs change in the future. Borrowing a tactic from the insurance industry, Avon sales rep now follow up with "orphan accounts" — customers whose previous sales rep is no longer active.

Under the heading "alumni relations," many companies apply this tactic to people as well. When your employees leave, they may swear allegiance to a competitor. But they may just as easily be new customer prospects for you. They know what you offer and how well you deliver. Instead of begrudging them the opportunity to improve their circumstances, use their familiarity to your own advantage.

98

Contact Lost Customers

99

Contact Silent Customers

Some customers are just too good to be true. They're a joy to do business with. They always seem to be satisfied. Their bills are invariably paid on time. They never voice a complaint. It's easy to lose track of them in the daily racket raised by other, more demanding customers. Don't. You don't want them taking their business elsewhere.

Set up systems that assure someone is in periodic contact with these bedrock accounts. And make sure they receive a little extra TLC if ever they do encounter a problem. Keep them feeling involved and valued and well-informed about your products and services. Survey them in-depth to determine the bonds that link them to you. Then work to find ways to duplicate those conditions to solidify other accounts.

100

Say 'Thank You'

The two most effective words in the English language when it comes to bringing customers back again are "Thank You." They've just given you their business, their trust, their money. In return, you've given them goods or services of commensurate value. If that's where the transaction ends, it may well be where the customer relationship ends.

Tell customers, verbally and in writing, that you appreciate having their business. For customers with whom you have a personal relationship, send handwritten thank-you notes after the service transaction is completed. Empower your people to develop their own relationships by providing time and resources for this kind of positive follow through. You can't wear those two words out. They get stronger every time you use them.

#101
PAY ATTENTION

A blinding flash of the obvious? Maybe. But it's easy to look for One Big Solution to the service quality challenge — and in service, bigger is not better. Sometimes bigger is irrelevant, but often it just gets in the way of all the crucial one-to-one interactions between a business and its customers that add up to an index of satisfaction or dissatisfaction.

Satisfied customers come back. Dissatisfied customers may not. If the point of being in business is to have customers again, then it's incumbent on every executive, manager, supervisor and frontline worker — whether in direct customer contact or in a supporting role deep within the organization — to make sure each and every customer contact is managed to the organization's advantage.

Everything counts for the customer — no *detail* is too small or insignificant. Everybody on the customer service team has an important role to play — no *person* is too small or insignificant, either.

Learn from everything you see, hear, read or experience. Good ideas come from a wide variety of sources. But if you're not looking for them, if you're not keeping track of each and every little detail, you won't recognize them.

Good service is the end product of all the big and little things your business does for its customers. From their standpoint, everything counts. Keep them satisfied, and they'll not only keep you in business, but put you way ahead of your competitors.

It's just a matter of taking care of business.

WANT MORE COPIES?

This and most other Lakewood books are available at special quantity discounts when purchased in bulk. For details write: Lakewood Books, 50 South Ninth Street, Minneapolis, MN 55402. Or call (800) 328-4329, (612) 333-0471.

MORE ON SERVICE QUALITY

Service America! Doing Business in the New Economy $19.95

The Service Edge: 101 Companies That Profit From Customer Care $19.95

Service Solutions: The Service Edge Newsletter's Best Thinking on Improving Service $19.95

Service Wisdom: Creating and Maintaining the Customer Service Edge $19.95

Total Quality: The Executive Guide to the New American Way of Doing Business $39.95

To charge your order or for quantity discounts, call (800) 328-4329 or (612) 333-0471. FAX: (612) 333-6526.

Mail orders to: Lakewood Books, 50 South Ninth Street, Minneapolis, MN 55402.